DANGER Down Under

AUSTRALIAN BOX JELLYFISH

by Rachel Rose

Minneapolis, Minnesota

Credits
Cover and title page, © Juergen Freund/Nature Picture Library, © Johan Holmdahl/iStock, and © BobHemphill/iStock; 4–5, © Gary Bell/Blue Planet Archive; 6, © Auscape International Pty Ltd/Alamy; 7, © Jurgen Freund/Minden; 9T, © Dr. David Wachenfeld/Minden; 9B, © Juergen Freund/Nature Picture Library; 10–11, © Gary Bell/ Oceanwide/Minden; 12, © Colin_Davis/iStock; 12–13, © Auscape International Pty Ltd/Alamy; 14, © ANT Photo Library/Science Source; 15, © Auscape/Getty Images; 16–17, © Michael Evans/Adobe Stock; 19, © Jurgen Freund/Minden; 20–21, © Dr. David Wachenfeld/Minden; 22, © David Fleetham/Alamy; 23, © thekovtun/Shutterstock.

Bearport Publishing Company Product Development Team
President: Jen Jenson; Director of Product Development: Spencer Brinker; Managing Editor: Allison Juda; Associate Editor: Naomi Reich; Associate Editor: Tiana Tran; Art Director: Colin O'Dea; Designer: Elena Klinkner; Designer: Kayla Eggert; Product Development Assistant: Owen Hamlin

STATEMENT ON USAGE OF GENERATIVE ARTIFICIAL INTELLIGENCE
Bearport Publishing remains committed to publishing high-quality nonfiction books. Therefore, we restrict the use of generative AI to ensure accuracy of all text and visual components pertaining to a book's subject. See BearportPublishing.com for details.

Library of Congress Cataloging-in-Publication Data

Names: Rose, Rachel, 1968- author.
Title: Australian box jellyfish / by Rachel Rose.
Description: Minneapolis, Minnesota : Bearport Publishing Company, [2024] | Series: Danger down under | Includes bibliographical references and index.
Identifiers: LCCN 2023030964 (print) | LCCN 2023030965 (ebook) | ISBN 9798889164975 (library binding) | ISBN 9798889165040 (paperback) | ISBN 9798889165101 (ebook)
Subjects: LCSH: Cubomedusae--Juvenile literature.
Classification: LCC QL377.S4 R66 2024 (print) | LCC QL377.S4 (ebook) | DDC 593.5/3--dc23/eng/20230712
LC record available at https://lccn.loc.gov/2023030964
LC ebook record available at https://lccn.loc.gov/2023030965

Copyright ©2024 Bearport Publishing Company. All rights reserved. No part of this publication may be reproduced in whole or in part, stored in any retrieval system, or transmitted in any form or by any means, electronic, mechanical, photocopying, recording, or otherwise, without written permission from the publisher.

For more information, write to Bearport Publishing, 5357 Penn Avenue South, Minneapolis, MN 55419.

CONTENTS

Deadly Sting........................4
Something Fishy....................6
Shallow Swimmers...................8
Thousands of Stings...............10
Got Ya!...........................12
Hunting Superpowers...............14
People Beware!....................16
Life Cycles.......................18
Back to Sea.......................20

More about Jellyfish..............22
Glossary..........................23
Index.............................24
Read More.........................24
Learn More Online.................24
About the Author..................24

DEADLY STING

Danger lurks in the waters Down Under.

A floating creature spies its next meal and quickly sets off. The Australian box jellyfish uses its long **tentacles** to catch a fish and deliver a deadly sting. Venom spreads, and the powerless fish is made into a meal.

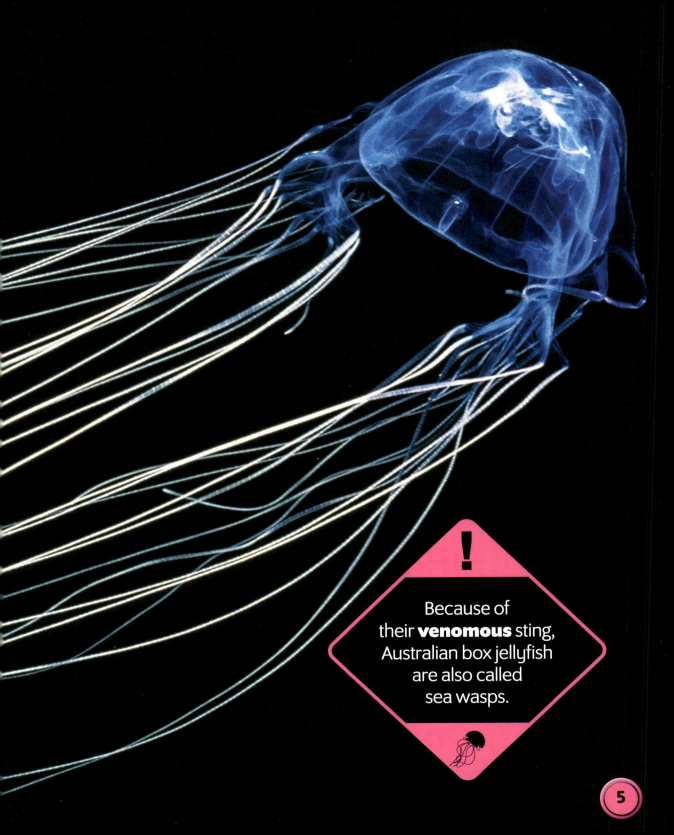

> **!**
> Because of their **venomous** sting, Australian box jellyfish are also called sea wasps.

SOMETHING FISHY

Box jellyfish get their names from the boxlike shape of their bodies. They look like floating cubes with thin legs. However, the *fish* part of their name isn't quite right. Jellyfish aren't actually fish. They are **invertebrates**. Their soft, jellylike bodies don't have backbones.

Box jellyfish are nearly **transparent**, which makes them hard to see in the water.

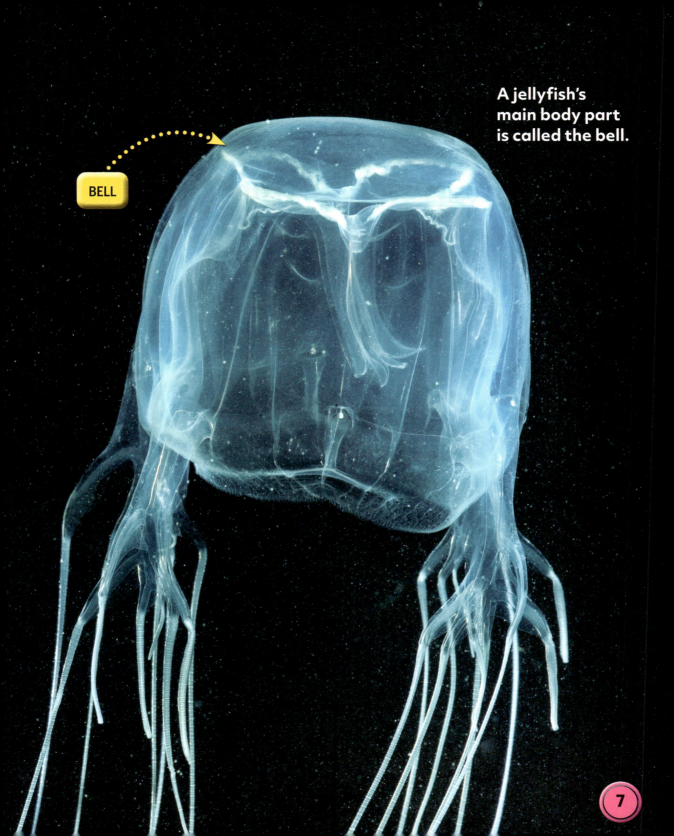

BELL

A jellyfish's main body part is called the bell.

7

SHALLOW SWIMMERS

There are more than 50 kinds of box jellyfish swimming in waters around the world, but Australian box jellyfish are the deadliest of all. In fact, these jellyfish are the world's most venomous **marine** animals. Australian box jellyfish are found mostly just off northern Australia. They prefer warm, coastal waters.

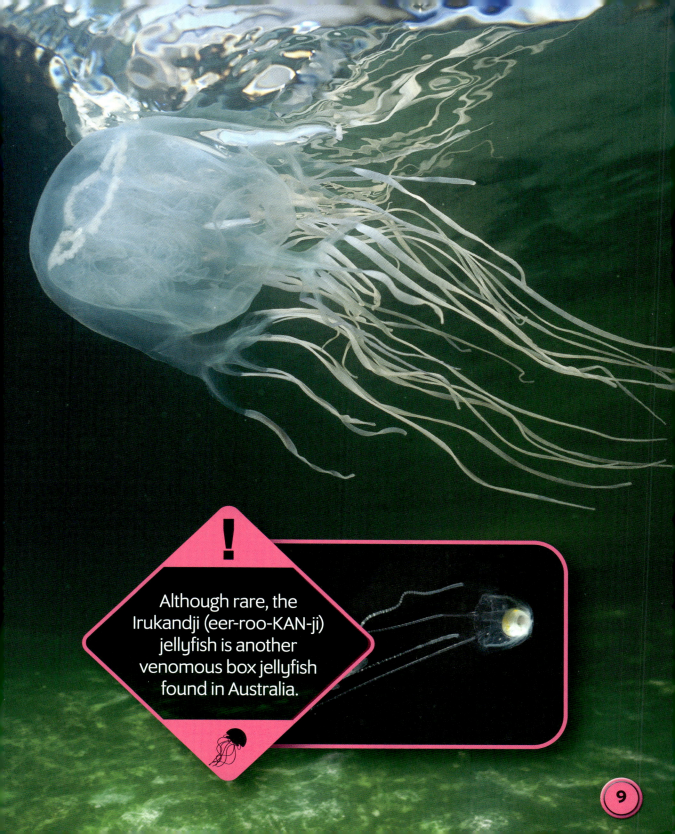

! Although rare, the Irukandji (eer-roo-KAN-ji) jellyfish is another venomous box jellyfish found in Australia.

THOUSANDS OF STINGS

The Australian box jellyfish is the largest of all box jelly **species**. It has about 60 tentacles that can each grow up to 10 feet (3 m) long. That's about as long as a kayak! But at least a kayak doesn't sting. Each tentacle has around 5,000 stinging cells that the ocean creature uses to protect itself or attack its **prey**.

> **!** Once the jellyfish's tentacle touches a creature, the stinging cells immediately shoot out mini needles filled with venom.

GOT YA!

Australian box jellyfish hunt mostly small fish, worms, and shrimp. Once they catch prey in their tentacles, the jellyfish sting it with venom. The toxic venom **stuns** the prey, making it unable to move and easier for the jellyfish to eat. Some creatures even die within minutes after being stung!

Some animals, such as sharks and green sea turtles, are not affected by box jellyfish venom.

A FISH CAUGHT BY A BOX JELLYFISH

HUNTING SUPERPOWERS

Venom isn't the only thing that makes Australian box jellyfish dangerous. Most jellyfish float, moving in whichever direction the water takes them. However, box jellyfish can control where they go. These jellies can swim almost 5 miles per hour (8 kph) through the water. In addition, while other jellyfish can only sense movement, box jellyfish have actual eyes to spot prey.

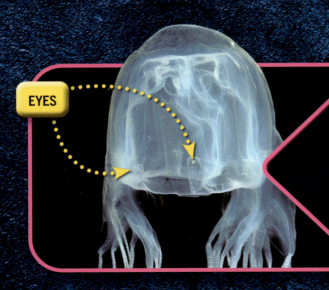

EYES

Box jellyfish have a total of 24 eyes, divided into groups of six eyes on each of the four sides of their body.

PEOPLE BEWARE!

Though they don't hunt humans, Australian box jellyfish are still something people should watch out for. Since these jellies prefer shallow waters, they are found close to where people like to swim. In the rare cases when people get stung, it can be extremely dangerous. Swimmers should watch out for signs warning about box jellyfish in the water.

!

Australian box jellyfish are most active during stinger season, which lasts from late October until May.

LIFE CYCLES

When box jellyfish are ready to **breed**, they make their way to inland waters, such as rivers and **estuaries**. These jellies lay their eggs in the water and die shortly after. The eggs soon hatch into tiny wormlike creatures and later become **polyps**. But their life cycle doesn't end there—they keep growing and growing until they become adult jellyfish.

As a polyp, a jellyfish can split itself in half and create another polyp!

POLYPS

BACK TO SEA

Once they have grown large enough, box jellyfish return to the sea. By then, their tentacles are ready to give a venomous sting, so stay back! These jellies will spend the rest of their lives swimming and stinging off the coast of Australia. Watch out for this danger Down Under!

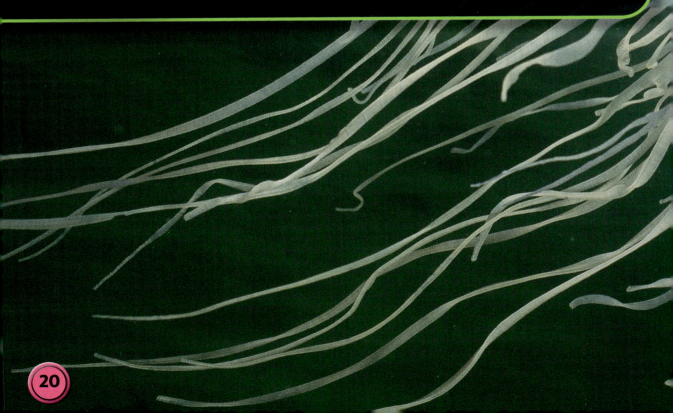

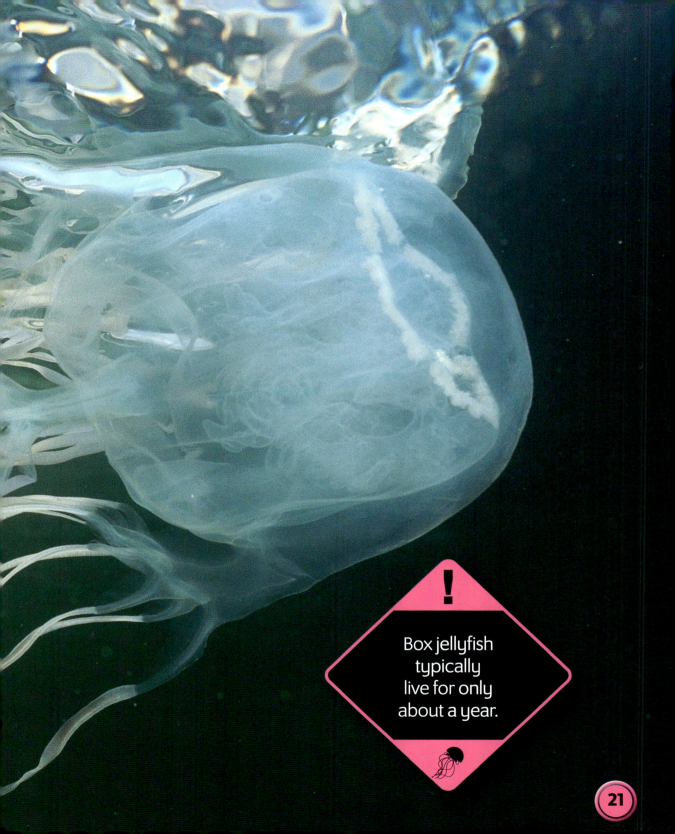

! Box jellyfish typically live for only about a year.

MORE ABOUT JELLYFISH

- ⚠ Another name for box jellyfish is marine stingers.

- ⚠ Box jellyfish usually breed during one time of the year.

- ⚠ There are more than 2,000 different kinds of jellyfish in the world.

- ⚠ Some kinds of jellyfish are as small as a thumbnail.

- ⚠ A jellyfish has a mouth and a stomach, but it doesn't have a heart or brain.

- ⚠ A box jellyfish has enough venom to kill up to 60 people within a few minutes.

- ⚠ If a box jellyfish doesn't eat for an entire day, it will start to get smaller.

GLOSSARY

breed to have young

estuaries coastal waters that are a mix of fresh water and salty ocean water

invertebrates animals that don't have a backbone

marine something that has to do with the sea

polyps tiny sea animals at the beginning stages of the jellyfish life cycle

prey animals that are hunted and eaten by other animals

species closely related groups of animals

stuns shocks something so much that it is unable to move

tentacles body parts that hang down from a jellyfish's body and can sting other animals

transparent able to be seen through

venomous full of poison that can be delivered to another animal by a sting or bite

Index

bell 7
breed 18, 22
coast 8, 20
invertebrates 6
ocean 10
prey 10, 12
rivers 18
species 10
sting 4–5, 10, 12, 16, 20, 22
tentacles 4, 10, 12, 20
venom 4–5, 8–10, 12, 14

Read More

Humphrey, Natalie. *Box Jellyfish vs. Asian Giant Hornet (Bizarre Beast Battles).* New York: Gareth Stevens, 2023.

Stratton, Connor. *Box Jellyfish (Deadliest Animals).* Mendota Heights, MN: Apex, 2023.

Learn More Online

1. Go to **www.factsurfer.com** or scan the QR code below.
2. Enter **"Australian Box Jellyfish"** into the search box.
3. Click on the cover of this book to see a list of websites.

About the Author

Rachel Rose writes books for kids and teaches yoga. Her favorite animal of all is her dog, Sandy.